This is the Dark Star.

The screen flickers on and Zardoz appears with a sinister grin.
He points to the exit.

Sure!
What will happen to them? What is waiting for them outside?

The door opens and they walk down the ramp. They are sure something bad is going to happen.

Don't push me! You creep!
That way, now! And step on it!

Wow! What wicked floodlights!
They are taken to a football pitch. It is in darkness, but soon floodlights come on and send a blinding light over the pitch. They gawk at what they see!

The pitch is amazing! They relax.
They want to play!

So ... they do just that!

Art hits a cross,
and Scooter heads it
straight into the net!

The ball comes hurtling towards Janaki. No problem! She tips it over the cross bar.

But do you think they can be the champions?
Oh yes, they are top class.

Then they stay on Dark Star. Lock them up with the rest.

Slam!
I had a feeling this was a trap.
O.K. So now what?